Overlove

Bernadette Malavarca

Made with ❤ on the BookLeaf Publishing Platform
www.bookleafpub.in
www.bookleafpub.com

Dedication

To my loves, on earth and beyond—thank you

Preface

This is an exploration of the loves—love between people, love for art, love for places, love for moments, and more —through twenty-one poems. Twenty-one, so few, so young. A sliver is here, but the exploration is endless.

Acknowledgements

Many thanks to all encounters and experiences.

1. Truth

I shake
In my boots
As I tell the truth

2. BOOM!

All the love! Such love!
Much love has passed through my chest doors,
which are like the ones of a saloon—never fully closed,
squeaking, with spring and swing, with initials and nicks
and splinters but holding up through the ages.

All the love that has passed through!
Like ocean breeze,
Like hurricane wind,
Like sheriffs coming off duty.

I am nothing but a vessel.

And one day—BOOM!
Back to cosmos.

3. November

November is a middle child
No mysticism of October
No sparkle of December
We have crossed over to cold and rain
The holidays chasing us down
We start running harder
Fighting the turned back clock
We near another year end
We did few things on the list
Our ambiguous dreams
And mysterious ailments persist
Mother-in-law still unsoftened
Politics still sci fi
True love remains a unicorn
We are tired
Want to wind down
Have that designated day of thanks
A strange custom
Ennui in our drunk eyes that roll over hills of beer bellies
in polo shirts on the couch
Sea of khaki
Cheers when grown men collide hitting helmets
Wrestling a ball

November is a ground of dead leaves
We walk mindlessly over the metaphor

4. Piano

5

Piano unlocks memories
Of you and me
In times not of our time
Lets me look
With eyes of soul
Visions clear
Of worlds
Beyond here

5. Open Hands

Love with open hands
No plans
No demands

6. Together

She taught me the woods
And I taught her the city
She taught me TV
And I taught her nightclubs
She taught me quiet
And I taught her loud
She taught me habit
And I taught her change
She taught me protection
And I taught her exposure
She taught me the head
And I taught her the heart
She taught me water
And I taught her wine
She taught me silly
And I taught her serious
She taught me to spar
And I taught her to spare
She taught me fearlessness
And I taught her caution
She taught me tough
And I taught her tender
Teachers
Students

Companions
We have lived
Life
Together

7. Friendship Express

Hey, hey
Let's go
To gardens
To museums
Over bridges
'Cross seas
Let's talk
Tell me true things
Show me shark bites
I love you, man,
And you, too,
Seriously
We are the sky
Prick our skin
Take my blood
Sorry about your dad
We all have our jobs
Funny how we met
What's our song?
Wish I'd known you then
The men come and go
Takes a secret word to board
The Friendship Express

8. Seymour Street

I understand that man and his cigarette, his confidante, the only one who gets his lips, and sits with him each morning outside the halfway house on Seymour Street. Holds on with him in the wind and validates his cough, a wolf howl into the sky.

9. Distortion

11

I drank the bourbon
To bury my pain
Cut the highs of my heart
And the lows of my loins
But it only turned them up
And added distortion

10. Track 14

If I stop and think about what it means to ride this train, really look at the greasy big machine, longer than my eyes can see, faster than my best estimate, loaded with strangers, powered by electricity and our trust day in and out on tracks through Secaucus, with a conductor who has a voice but no face, if I really thought about it, all the seats would come apart, the gears would come undone, I wouldn't know what it means to "board" or "depart" or "arrive,"

. . . but it just becomes what you do.

If I really thought about it, this living life with you, the belly of my entire world exposed, mixing with your skin, this trusting the coordination of our dreams over time, trusting that our hearts will stay at the very least in tact, if I thought about all we put on the line, I might cover myself with these lovers' sheets and run afraid into the stone hills of invulnerability

. . . but it just becomes what you do.

If I really thought about it, that I eat each day, more than

once, that I have a ten-dollar bill in my pocket, that I am
in a two-car family, that I have working eyes and heart,
that I have possessions for pleasure alone—my books, my
beach blanket, my candles, my Hudson bourbon—that I
graze on tapas while there are babies in cages, I might
freeze and collapse in my living room, or scream in the
middle of the dance floor, ceasing my go-abouts

. . . but it just becomes what you do.

If I really thought about the businessmen I pass each day
who step over the homeless men, hundreds at once in
the city, feet over bodies every minute, that every other
homeless man is a schizophrenic in a system that can't
hold yet another of him, that despite this, I need to clock
in, if I really thought about it, the ties on the necks of the
merchants would melt into a goo like in a Dalí, the
sidewalk would cave into the center of the earth, which
would turn out to be black space with all of us floating,
particles together alone

. . . but it just becomes what you do.

11. Miraculous

Miraculous, the sky
Miraculous, the night
Miraculous, fire,
Miraculous, this breeze
Miraculous, your face
Miraculous, this kiss
Miraculous, this house
Miraculous, the highway
Miraculous, the Redwood
Miraculous, the maiden,
Miraculous, the crone,
Miraculous, the rain
Miraculous, melody,
Miraculous, harmony,
Miraculous, beat,
Miraculous, dancing
Miraculous, Italy,
Miraculous, New York,
Miraculous, Maine,
Miraculous, Asbury,
Miraculous, bear,
Miraculous, bumble bee,
Miraculous, love,
Miraculous, the sea,

Miraculous, tulip,
Miraculous, lemon tree,
Miraculous, burgundy,
Miraculous, Malbec,
Miraculous, cells,
Miraculous, breath,
Miraculous, voice,
Miraculous, mind,
Miraculous, language,
Miraculous, sight,
Miraculous, tears,
Miraculous, touch,
Miraculous, cumming,
Miraculous, conception,
Miraculous, baby cry,
Miraculous, community,
Miraculous, memory,
Miraculous, impermanence,
Miraculous, eternity,
Miraculous, entirety,
Miraculous, Debussy,
Miraculous, sandalwood,
Miraculous, mountain,
Miraculous, paths crossing,
Miraculous, meeting you

12. Pandemic Rain

Pitter
Patter
Paradiddles pound puddles,
Pours—the rain

Pandemic rain

The wind led up to this
lulling storm,
blew pedals off cherry blossom
trees today
all-over pink

Pandemic pink

Tonight I turn in at nine
sink into stillness
under covers with my
longings and questions,
loves and quandaries
on pause in quarantine
my dread and my dreams

Pandemic dreams

Inner chide: "Use the time!"
this strange time
I watch from my window
the systems collapse
uncertainty ubiquitous
How can we begin again,
sift the mud and find the gems?

Pandemic gems

13. All That's Real

Before I die, I will shoot my best arrow. Aiming true. I will surrender to my call. And if the music kills me, so be it.

Before I die, I will see Ireland. Drink whiskey and sing with the locals in the pub. Kiss you on the green.

Before I die, I will hold my mothers hands in silence. Put all our humanness behind us.

Before I die, I will host a feast for my friends. The endless meal. Give them glee. Honor my soul family with wine, laughter, and song.

Before I die, I will meditate on the Sunset Cliffs. Take spirit in from the Pacific.

Before I die, I will learn to cook. Slowly. Savoring. Belaboring. For a family.

Before I die, I will give one million kisses away, embrace one million babes, release one million tears, pet one million animals, encourage one million children.

Before I die, let me say thank you. To all my teachers.
This has been something.

Before I die, I will leave a summary. The point is, what I
meant to say was...

All that's real is Love.

14. Never, Us, Will I Forget

Too late to change a single thing
But I'll make beauty of this suffering
A melody to melt the pain
A line, a beat, a sweet refrain,
Not "goodbye" but "see you later"
In dreams and sky and reflective waters
In baby smiles and puppy eyes
In butterflies and fireflies
In songs and films and hardbound books
In corridors and hidden nooks
Of our ancient souls when we're alone
In the darkest rooms of our separate homes
Neither of us knowable completely
We met, adjoined, and are now releasing
For better or worse; a blessing and curse
But layered, rich—a sutra verse
Perhaps some things we do regret,
But, never, us, will I forget

15. New York

Keep me busy till I die, City,
With curry and Korean and the Bowery and bridges and
cabbies
And paintings and pimps and princesses
And hobos and venture capitalists and aging professors
in rent-controlled apartments
And rats and bikes and knock-off bags and stairwells and
garbage and lights and lovers
And loneliness and busking and buses and traffic and
madness
And everyone in the center of everything and anonymity
and nicotine and horse manure
And the moon over filthy water

16. Drop

Howling and reluctant,
I tumbled
from a tired woman
into the world—
like a bead of blood
into a water jar—
and dissipated.

Love and art
whisk the liquid—
I nearly congeal
but never return to
a pure drop.

Was deep, hot red,
then thin, cool pink,
translucent,
all the while,
evaporating.

17. American Day

The smile of a passing dog,
suburban afternoon,
worn, wandering,
taking paces in my American day.

Mothers crowd the square,
nannies trail behind them,
children zip and zoom,
high on caffeine dreams.

All roads closed,
smartphone says so,
newspapers cling to newsstands,
obsolete like milkmen.

Snowflakes,
unrepeatable structures
fall in the predictable day,
melt on my eyelids,
I watched as long as I could.

Dream shards
poke through
this winter blanket,

fire flies in the mundane jar
rapid fire in the igloo.

18. Soul Surgeon

Soul surgeon
Into me
Intimate
Gazes,
effortless,
precise
incisions,
excavate
my confessions.

Don't tell
on me, how soft I am.

Heal me,
my teacher,
my Virgil, goddamn.
Been waiting,
troubled by maps
upside down.
Was never good
with directions, direction
rulers, rules,
orders, order.
"supposed tos"—

nebulous,
loose on the hips,
tight on the chest.

Your focus,
a spotlight,
I squirm but surrender,
transfixed,
seen.

In so quick,
then out.

You can't just go,
truncate,
interrupt
mid-pull.
We were just beginning,
talking universe,
and gridlessness,
art and assholes,
and brand new ways . . .

Next time,
by the sea,
with hot drinks and no clocks.

19. I Don't Know

I don't know what a poet is,
but here's a page with my blood on it .
I don't know who the artists are,
but I made you something.
I don't know if there's a God,
but sometimes I see ghosts.

I don't know what success is,
but I think we're doing okay with these Korean tacos in
Asbury,
I don't know what they mean by "be hungry,"
but I feel pretty full every day.
I don't know what he wants with "more aggressive,"
but it seems rude to interrupt people.

I don't know my party,
but that guy is a dick.
I don't know if some sex is a sin,
but it's none of your business.
I don't know if women are weak,
but we bleed while giving speeches.

I don't know what tolerance means,
but holidays back home feel icy.

I don't know about holy unions,
but this love has burrowed in my bone marrow.
I don't know what forever is,
but I'd like this to keep going.

20. Wild Lilies

Wild lilies
burst orange
along West Hurley
under a cloudless sky
on the Fourth of July—
epitome
of free.

21. Overlove

Overlove
Is what I'm dying of
I try my best to keep it all in my chest
But then it comes—
A sea of salty tears
A million blazing suns
I hold them all right here
For my dears—
Overlove

Overlove
Is what I'm dying of
If you come to my home
And all that's left are my bones
Then you'll know—
She's left you for the sky
Back to cosmos
Where the angels fly
Couldn't bear
Overlove

There's a hole in my chest
I'm a mess, I confess
I apologize

I don't mean to be hurtful
You can go
You can stay
Rail against all I say
And it's still okay—
Wouldn't change how I see you
Love is slow
Love is kind
Love is edgeless and divine
Love is wine
And I spill my cup on you
I sleep outside your window
Singing, "O Sole Mio,"
Is that fine,
Or obsessed and reckless?

Overlove
Is what I'm dying of